The Winter Planting

THE WINTER PLANTING

A long year's repentance

By

Keith Stuhler

First Edition

"We are all broken. That's how the light gets in,"
said Ernest Hemingway.

Some are more broken than others, Mr. Hemingway.
The light at first blinds those long in despair.
At first, so brightly, we could not see.
Our minds resist.
If we are to heal, it must come from the heart.

Introduction

|

I struggle to write this story, not because I lack the desire, but because I am not a writer by trade. Yet I am compelled to share the story of a transformational life experience.

Some would say the old man who had existed before finding God had simply lived according to other people's expectations. I completed college, played twelve years of professional golf with everything that life entailed, traveled to many places in this world, had wonderful creative business experiences, and had my family's unconditional love. Still, none of these things brought me true contentment.

Most did not know the fears, insecurities, and hopelessness that had plagued my life. Two of the diagnoses were severe depression and clinical anxiety. Few knew about my solutions to those afflictions. I hid those solutions well. By seeking relief from my plagues of depression and anxiety through drugs, I found only isolation and shame. I came to see death as an inevitable end, one that made every accomplishment feel futile.

I walked well. I talked well. Outwardly, I appeared steady. But there was nothing there.

My reason for sharing this story is simple: if even one person finds a measure of the freedom, contentment, and clarity of mind that God has given me, then putting these words to paper will have been worth it.

About This Writing

I sit next to Andy on my porch in Pompano Beach, thinking how pretty she is. We laugh out loud about something stupid. I look at the harbor and think about the day two years ago when I left a place called Faith Farm. The change in me has been profound. I have truly become a new man. A free man. A man with purpose.

All of us recognize the catastrophic failures in our lives, but there are also the subtle, perceived failures only the person can see and feel. Maybe a glance from someone that you took the wrong way, a comment by a loved one that you misunderstood. They shape you. They wear on you. They are insidious and can last a lifetime. It becomes a life of never feeling quite good enough, of merely getting by. Never reaching what God intended. Seeing it, tasting it but never receiving the contentment of finding it.

This is the story of my journey from depression, anxiety, loneliness, and drug addiction. It is the miraculous story of my evolution from a purposeless life to one filled with meaning. It is my journey from atheism to faith. It is a story of endurance and transformation, of lost love and discovery. It tells how my life changed at an age many would consider near its end rather than its beginning.

It is the story of finding God at an age and in a place I never expected. It's about how God revealed Himself to me at 73 years old and how that experience felt from my perspective. I did not go to this place called Faith Farm looking for God. I went there looking for a place to hide. Maybe even a place to die and just disappear from life. I certainly was not looking for change. I was convinced I was okay with the way I was and that it was others who were off.

I wanted nothing to do with the imaginary god of Faith Farm. I thought I would play their game in exchange for shelter, food, and a chance to gather myself, but God had other plans for me. He dropped me into that place of change. He freely gave me forgiveness, healing, restoration, and clarity of mind. At first, I thought these were things I did not need.

My story is, at its core, a simple gratitude—my very personal account written for those who have their own plagues and demons and may have dismissed spirituality as simple folklore as I did.

If you are an atheist, if you are a drug addict, if you are lost in life, whether you are old or young, God will meet you where you are. He can and will restore a corrupted soul. I believe this because He restored mine.

Hopefully, my story helps you feel what my year at Faith Farm was like. So much of my transformation came from feelings and emotions. Not intellectual or rational insights. It was a year of pure feelings. It was a year lived almost entirely through emotion. There were no TVs, internet, cell phones, or newspapers. No distractions. No leaving the farm physically or mentally for one year.

I discovered things about my true self—some good, some ugly—but all honest. I had always hungered for that insight into myself but had never been on a path to self-awareness. God hurled me onto His path. It was not an easy one.

There would be no fluff at this farm. There was no weaning or detoxing of any kind, either from the substances that had taken hold of me or from my old ways of being. Everything had to be left at the door.

The Faith Farm is a Christian regeneration work program. It benefits homeless, tertiary drug addicts, and alcoholics. I read in the farm's pamphlet that stated: *Ours is not a twelve-step program about rehabilitation. It is a one-step program toward God. We will show you how to move from a pretentious, superficial existence to freedom. Your perspective will change if you are willing.* Here was the rub. What did they mean "willing?" Reflexively, I said that I was willing, but I did not really know the depth of that commitment. I would learn what that meant.

One might conclude that being in such an intense environment for a long year would lead anyone to blindly accept all that was presented and automatically change. But I believe that true change can only be achieved voluntarily, without coercion.

A commitment to follow that narrow path is something else. A willingness to change is tricky; all do not accept it. Each man wrote his own transformation or non-transformation story of his time at the farm. We were not, however, the authors of our stories.

To repent is to change, to leave one's own way and to follow His way. This is the path to true freedom. I took His path, and I found my freedom. It was a gradual opening to change throughout my journey on His path, and that gradual sense of need propelled me and was my salvation.

My story follows from my arrival to my graduation. I did my part, but I could not have changed on my own. God was the author and the director of my transformation. He is that bridge at Faith Farm that connects us to Him, to ourselves, to each other, and to our destiny. He is a bridge over a bridge.

There was an unfamiliar voice that spoke to me throughout my time at the farm, providing encouragement. I started to hear it as soon as my head began to clear. Looking back, I now know that voice was the Holy Spirit softly speaking to me though my corrupted soul encouraged me, rooted me on.

CHAPTER ONE

How the hell did I wind up at a farm for the homeless

After graduating from college with a degree in Russian Studies I became a golf professional, dating my future wife Andrea (Andy) in the mid-seventies while practicing in Florida. We had pure fun but drifted apart. For fifteen years we lived our separate lives. She married and moved to Maryland. I stayed in the golf profession as a club pro, playing some minor league tours for another ten years. I got married and had a beautiful son.

I am ashamed to say I became a drug addict during those years, for which I hold only myself to blame. After golf, I owned various companies while deep in my addiction. Pure restlessness drove me from one venture to the next. A drug addict never finds contentment or satisfaction with anything.

I think I was trying to find some kind of inspiration after the highs of my golf career. My efforts only fueled my drug addiction.

I got divorced during those years. Fortunately, I still shared custody of my son, who I loved as much as a self-centered drug addict was capable of. Today I love him unconditionally.

In the spring of 1990, I walked into a West Palm Beach restaurant, and I heard her unmistakable laugh. Andy looked as beautiful as she was fifteen years earlier. We immediately connected and were together again. We have been married for thirty-four years. I was an addict for thirty-one of those years. She saw something in me that I could not and has always been an encouragement to me.

From the time we first met, I remember telling her she had a pure soul, not really knowing what that meant then. The fact that she has stayed with me for all those years is a testament to her extraordinary loyalty and capacity to love.

After bouncing around various golf tours, with stints as a club pro, I ended my golf career. I started a technology company promoting a new innovation: golf simulators. Headquartered in Silicon Valley, I traveled extensively, promoting, selling, and expanding the applications of the devices, both in the U.S. and internationally. I eventually caught the interest of some major Japanese investors. After several trips to Singapore and Tokyo they agreed to fully capitalize my venture.

They later withdrew their offer saying that I was "of low moral character." I was depressed, drug addicted and denied God. They were not wrong.

Returning on the long flight from Tokyo in 1999, with their words echoing in my mind, I resolved to become a better person. But how do I do that? Quit my affair with drugs? That was obvious answer but not the one I chose.

My solution to my moral failure? I decided I would volunteer to teach golf to special education children in Palm Beach County schools. I convinced myself I could redeem my character by doing good for others. I believed doing charitable deeds would make me a better person—no God, still drug addicted, still depressed but in other's eyes a "good person." That was my plan, and I was excited about it.

I spent the next two years on dusty school playgrounds. In reality, I was simply offering encouragement to mentally challenged kids—just being kind to another person. Simply that. It felt right for a while. But soon my ambition kicked in, and I lost my plan of redemption. I lost my way again.

I helped turn a small, disorganized foundation into a successful national charity, became C.E.O., designed and oversaw the construction of a unique golf course designed specifically for mentally and physically challenged children—the first of its kind in the world. I also developed a professional golf teaching program for the facility to give the kids experiences they never thought possible.

The objective was never to create good golfers but to give these kids a look at what self-esteem might feel like for a person who had never experienced it.

That irony wasn't lost on me. These children were learning self-esteem by a man who had none. Nonetheless, there I was, addressing my students about preparedness equaling confidence and the like.

The facility opened to national recognition in 2001. I later added a disabled veteran and an inner-city kids' program to fully utilize the facilities. I was "doing good" and lauded for my work. I would deliver speeches to well-heeled donors and celebrities in the morning, do a television interview in the afternoon and smoke crack cocaine in the clubhouse till dawn by myself.

I received validation from the media and others, clearly receiving the worldly redemption I had sought, but it meant nothing to me. There was something missing. I was having my ego constantly puffed up, but that gave me no satisfaction. There I was a functioning addict, an actor playing the role of benefactor, nothing more. I was without God's grace.

After an injury during the construction of the golf facility, my drug choice shifted from cocaine to powerful pain meds, strong muscle relaxers, narcotic sleep aids, and anxiety meds. Eventually, psychotropic depression meds were added to my prescription list for my worsening depression.

After twelve years of generous support from donors and volunteers, their support dried up. The economy went into a recession, and the donors no longer had discretionary funds. Unable to make payroll, I rationalized that since I was the Foundation's creator, support was owed to me. It was so typical of me to lie to myself, instead of facing that reality head on. I used foundation funds to keep my family and my addiction going. It was the end for me and the Foundation. In disgrace from my actions and having no respect for myself or anyone else, we left our comfortable Palm Beach Gardens home and moved to a tiny condo in Boynton Beach.

the exile

In Boynton I became a boozy observer of my life, numbing my shame. Hiding from my disgrace. I was no longer actively participating in my life.

Shame, guilt, and perceived failure are the fuel for the drug addict's fire. I was an intense oil fire that was not easily put out.

Living in an over fifty-five condo community populated by retirees, I settled into a shadow life, numbing myself with serious pain medications, potent muscle relaxers, marijuana, anxiety meds and narcotic sleep aids. Anything that my doctor friend would prescribe. Droning on to anyone who would listen about who I used to be. Out of sight to everyone who had been meaningful to me before my disgrace. I spent the next ten years in exile. I took a series of low-level jobs that did not require sober intent. I soon lost my ability to create new opportunities because I was busy pretending to be something I was not. I was hiding from others what I believed was a failed self. I resented my wife and family for not pulling me out of my misery, even though I never spoke about it. Most of all, resenting myself, for who I had become, the drug numb exile, slowly suffocating, staring at the television for days on end refusing to even think about what got me there in the first place. I continued my drug use. I had no clarity of thought because I was constantly drug numb.

The neighbor in the next condo was a retired pastor and acquaintance. One day I looked for any kind of solace or advice from him. He was saying something, his lips were moving, he seemed sincere, but I was deaf to his words. He recommended some scripture and said God could guide and heal me if I let Him. I thought to myself yeah, heal me from what? The Bible sat on my coffee table with some parts highlighted. I never opened the book. My salvation was next door. I could have found enlightenment right then. I could at least have been comforted, but I was in my exile; I was not ready. I needed to be brought to my knees and completely surrendered before I could change. I was a stubborn type.

The ten-year exile ended with a delusion involving a financial and geographic cure. We sold everything we owned, furniture, and cars. We moved to Oklahoma City. It was a half-cooked business venture. Nothing went right there. It was a failure from the beginning. My drug use was around the clock. Andy was the only good thing I had left. In frustration she told me she was leaving me. She tried to talk to me when I had a moment of relative clarity. She said Keith "don't you believe in God?" I mumbled "of course not, you know I don't." "Keith, I think you're soul sick. I think that's your problem." "That's nonsense Andy but if I search for God would you stay and help me?" "Nope. I feel that you must find Him yourself," she said through her tears.

She had not given up on me even though I had given up on myself several years before. She simply could not watch me destroy myself anymore. She knew who I was inside and seeing me, as I was, hurt her too much. At the gate in the OKC airport before turning her back and walking to the plane she said, "Keith, I will always love you." As I walked toward the airport exit, I mumbled "always love you too" to no one. I did not know what real love was then but I would learn. She did what she had to do, and I will always love and respect her for that. It was the kindest thing she could have done. She was God's instrument in putting me on my long, dusty path to salvation. At the time I did not see any path, I just thought well, another life betrayal. My ego took the hit, and I was resentful. The only searching I did in Oklahoma was for a local doctor who would prescribe stronger pain medication and a medical marijuana card. One week later I abandoned everything we owned in the rented apartment. I faked a heart attack and when the EMTs picked me up I told them I had bad thoughts. The ambulance took me directly to Saint Anthony's Psychiatric unit in Oklahoma City. I received a diagnosis of major depressive disorder and generalized anxiety disorder.

An alternate diagnosis: "This patient is chronically soul sick. His future is bleak." I would not have understood that then, except for the bleak part.

what rock bottom looks like

|

I did not have a friend in this world. I am an alone 73-year-old. My wife left me. My son doesn't want or need me. My family pity me. I grieve the losses. For the first time in my life, I felt old. I was broken in every way possible. Curiously, without any familiar comforts, I felt a sense of freedom. I grabbed onto that thought and kept it close. It was the only positive I could find, and I so desperately needed one.

I have known fatherhood, college, P.G.A tournament golfer, and business owner. I have been a privileged traveler to many places in the world. So, I have had these life experiences. They would do me no good. I am broken, depressed, reliant on medications, delusional, and soul sick. I am fresh from three months in state psychiatric hospitals in Oklahoma and Florida, in which I willingly enlisted in clinical depression medication trials to get the pain drugs I was addicted to. I have always had a depressive nature, so it was not surprising that I was diagnosed that way. These trials involved non-F.D.A. approved medications to treat depression. "The study will take five weeks, we don't know the side effects and we're not promising a cure" said the doctor to me casually. "Will I still get my pain medication?" I said, trying to return his clinical tone. "Yes," he said. "In that case, I'm in." It seemed like a good deal.

At that point I felt that I had nothing and didn't really care where I was. It was a place to stay with food. I did not consider the negatives. My only real concern was that I would be provided with enough pain medication consistently.

I do not know if it was the pervasiveness of the drugs, or the environment and it does not really matter but I became delusional fast. I woke up one morning in a Florida psychiatric hospital after another restless night. My fellow patient and roommate did not look like he had left his bed in days. Wild hair, remnants of last night's spaghetti dinner still clinging to his hospital gown. I told him I had concluded that this place was a secret training location for senior Toyota executives. I hesitated then asked him if he agreed with that. "Yes, it is," he confirmed. Ok, good, at least I'm not crazy. I remember saying that out loud. I thought this as I was wearing an oversize, floral print hospital gown, size 4XL, and my primary residence was on the fifth floor of a state psychiatric hospital. I continued to engage my roommate; "you do know that these so-called nurses are stealing time from us while we sleep," pointing to the room clock. "Yeah, they got two hours from me last night." Looking back, I really am not sure what I meant about the nurses stealing time, but I remember believing it and feeling shorted by a couple of hours. So it went, over three months, in two state psychiatric hospitals.

After my insurance ran out, I left (was thrown out) of my final psychiatric hospital. My brother and Andy sent me a few dollars. I got a room at the cheapest motel I could find. Motel Six in Lantana, Florida. I sat on the edge of an unmade bed, with my face in my hands for one full day. I had the curtains shut, so the flickering TV was the only light in that seedy motel room. They did have complementary coffee, and I had enough medication from the hospital to keep me from severe withdrawal. I stayed there for a couple of days. Eventually, I got to the point when I had enough money for just one more night's rent and some food. I did not know what I would do then.

When I looked out the bathroom window, I could see several homeless men in the alley, and I pictured myself among them. I picked out a spot between a tree and a dumpster. That wouldn't be too bad; I'd be ok there. I think I was trying to convince myself, but it didn't take. The thought of living on a street took hold of me, and I was terrified by that possible reality. I saw them again when I walked across the street to the Quick Stop Haitian Market and looked away quickly.

If I bought a lottery ticket, I could win several million dollars. I dreamed briefly about how I would take the lump sum payment option; I would show everyone that I was really a successful guy after all.

That I had done things my way and came out well and that they had been wrong for doubting me. I bought five tickets instead of food. I was hoping for a miracle. The numbers did not hit. I did get my miracle that night, and the exile was over. I did not know it yet.

I walked back to the room. I was hungry and bought a Snickers bar in the motel vending machine. I tried to sleep with absolutely no idea how I could pay the next night's rent. At two in the morning, the phone woke me up. It was an angel disguised as Andy. A place would take me. It's called Faith Farm. It's two miles away. Go there. God had me. I didn't feel it.

I walked to the Faith Farm that next morning. I strained to get a first glimpse through the morning fog at the place that would be my new "home." The first thing that came into focus was a concrete bridge.

the bridge

|

My planting season is over. Nothing grows in cold soil... every man knows that. No sense in planting now. It's over for me; this winter season must be my time to die. I am afraid.

I arrived at the farm that morning. The vibe was not the Florida of sunny beaches and souvenir shops but something entirely different, rural agriculture, more like the cane fields of mid Florida than the high-rise condos that populated the coast. The Farm sat on a flat, swampy ninety-acre rectangle property.

It is defended on each side by fetid, algae-clogged moats with a hundred-foot bridge to the farm buildings arching over the western moat. The bridge has silver railings, and plain concrete sides. It is the only way in or out of the farm. Oddly, it is the farm's most well-built structure. It sits just off highway 441 and is easily visible from both directions. It is a solid concrete and rebar structure, intended to last longer than the many men who have walked over it in the past 75 years. A small, greenish, oxidized plaque memorializes the many nameless men whose lives were saved there.

Fittingly, the bridge's name is Hope Bridge. On the side of the bridge is the name FAITH FARM stamped in faded blue letters for all to see and understand what this place is. You can see the bridge from everywhere on the farm. It is intentionally the only way in or out of the property. It might as well be a twenty-mile-long causeway leading to an isolated island in the middle of the ocean. The farm is by design, totally detached from the world.

If it were possible for a gaunt, broken man to see then, how his perception of life would change when he walked the other way, one year later, he would have had a lighter, less cautious step. But unlike most journeys that are planned, I had no expectations of an outcome. I did not know what my future would be or if there was a future at all. I was sick and afraid. I would make this journey without any human support. I was very aware that I was on my own. I walked over the bridge with alert eyes and a tense body. I remember thinking Andy was sure right about one thing—I had to do this myself.

"Over de bridge" is the term used by the "students" when staying or leaving the farm. "He came from de bridge" (new guy) "he went out de bridge or he took de bridge" (quit or thrown out) into promised uncertainty.

I would frequently look at that bridge and daydream about another life, to be out of that place.

At first, I would dream of being drug thrilled, reliving that chemical euphoria of a drug high. That passed after a couple of months. Sometimes I would play out a comforting thought of happiness. It was a vague place that I could never quite pinpoint in my mind. It was always a generalized locale, calm and free from stress and worry and the weather was perfect (73, dry slight breeze). I'd sit on the grass and let the sun warm my face. I began to accept the fact that to get to that calm place I first had to "do" the bridge, front and back. You are either coming or going.

One day, maybe the second month in, while looking at that bridge, I made a conscious decision to stay and face the harsh realities that I would have run from in the past. The harshest reality I faced was not being in a cruddy environment but the realization that doing things my way had not worked. That was not an easy acceptance for a seventy-three-year-old man who had fleeting successes in his life. If I had made the wrong choices repeatedly, was I just a stupid fool without hope conditioned to make the same mistakes over and over? Maybe, just a bad person? After living for all those years, wasn't I supposed to know? I did not know. I had to find out who I was in this world. An unusual task for an old man. I made a commitment to myself to find out and this was the perfect place and time to do that. Was it coincidence that put me here at this time with these questions? The atheist thought so.

All those who have walked in over the bridge must leave a part of themselves that they thought they loved behind. If we go out over the bridge before graduating statistics say it is to relapse.

Six people I knew died of overdoses or were incarcerated after leaving the program early. That was just in the year I was at the Farm.

Crossing the bridge was a big deal. Is it even possible for a person to purge himself of a lifelong self-image? Stay or leave. Always the bridge. There is no pretending it's not there. If you're at the farm it is always right in front of you. It is a choice to stay and endure for one year, a loss of your old view of yourself and adopt a new one. Forget the enormous pull of the drugs, that's gone in a couple of months of abstention in most addicts. It's staying in an environment with no distractions and enduring painful personal truths. That's the hard part. "Stayin on the right side of that bridge."

I clearly remember the day when I asked myself, "can my ego be destroyed without attacking me, making matters worse?" And who is *me* anyway?

There it was. With this thought I had stumbled upon that major existential question. *Who am I?*

I had danced around this many times in my life but simply never had a framework to conclude anything. But could that question be answered in this dump, and at seventy-three. If it could, what a bonus that would be.

The only thing I knew for sure was that I was desperate. Making that choice to stay or walk away was my first faith leap. I understood, right from git. If I could embrace the symbolism of that damn bridge, I would be ok. I understood that the bridge represented a commitment to change. The bridge would be a symbol of the choice that God put in front of me. To repent or not, to change or not, I could walk over it at any time.

As God would tell me during the year "I do not give hope I am hope."

He did not just show me that bridge, He had me walk it, going both ways. It was something I related to right from the start of my journey. I cursed that bridge many times until I blessed it for saving me.

the farm

|

*My planting season is over. Nothing
grows in cold soil... every man knows
that. No sense in planting now. It's over
for me; this winter season must be my
time to die. I am afraid. —I wrote those
words on my first night. Little did I know.*

The "Farm" is not a traditional farmstead; it didn't grow corn or raise livestock. To call it a farm is to mislead of its intent.

There were no fields of crops growing in rows, no fallow fields, and no grazing sheep. Instead, it is operated as a thrift store enterprise with a mission to save people who are addicted to substances and are homeless. Keeping them sober. Feeding them. Getting them into a disciplined work routine. Letting them rest. Most importantly, showing them where to find God's love and teaching them Christian principles of life.

By everyone's definition, being a "student" at this farm was an option only when all other options are gone. The farm is home to fifty homeless drug addicts and alcoholics housed and fed in a large barracks. Many have been committed there from jails and prisons, some banished there by their families. No one has come there on their own. These men are the work force. To stay at this farm, you must work.

The farm supports its mission by being a functioning commercial enterprise. A thrift store selling donated furniture, appliances, clothing and bric-a-brac. Students from the farm drive box trucks to collect unwanted furniture, TVs, mattresses, clothing, and other items, often the remnants of lives left behind, from people who have died or are moving to a different stage in their lives.

The donations are picked up from two affluent counties for resale in the store. The Farm is a depository for things no longer wanted. Both discarded possessions and sick souls. Like all the others coming to Faith Farm, I was soul sick. As is each person in his own way.

Victor Frankel said, "when we no longer can change our situation, we must change ourselves." I believe that when we cannot change ourselves, we must discover who can. Since I couldn't change myself, I was looking for someone who could. I never imagined that I would find an omniscient loving presence who would guide me to profound change in that place, but I did.

I was surprised by the eagerness of my compatriots, born from desperation, to try to make sense of what was presented and look for a chance to change. I saw firsthand that a thirsty man whether he is old or young, will drink eagerly.

the daily farm life

|

My daily life at the farm was a constant search for relief from the crushing monotony. To stay at the farm, you must work. Workdays went by fast as they were days of activity. Sundays and holidays were filled with our attempts to make the time pass. They were long days. There were a few diversions. Writing to Andy, journaling, an occasional revelation, and smoking in a place called the smoke pit.

The smoke pit was a lean-to structure attached to the main barracks/dining building and adjacent to several dumpsters in the back alley. The smell of the tobacco smoke damped the stench of the dumpsters. It was the only place smoking was allowed on the farm. The smoke pit was the town square, so to speak. It was as close to being a social experience as the farm had.

The staff dictated that there would be no talking in the pit but that rule was largely ignored. It was there that new guys were thoughtfully evaluated, the latest gossip was shared, and rumors passed along. It wasn't important whether rumors were true or not. Good rumors were much valued and were passed along with enthusiasm. Letters from home were shared along with the sadness and happiness they carried. It was a good place for me to rekindle a smoking habit. I enjoyed my time being in the smoke pit.

For fifty men there were four toilets three urinals, five sinks and six working shower stalls at one end of barracks. The bathroom area was always busy in the morning with guys in underwear shaving and doing morning things. What a way to start the day. I was humbled every morning.

My personal changes were transformative, but they came over such large chunks of time that I could not really see them day by day. Each day on the farm was identical.

Two-inch thick, well-worn, foam pads served as mattresses, thrown on metal spring bunks which squeaked every time you rolled over. When they turned off the lights at ten p.m. you could not make out a shape from three feet away, I mean, the world just stopped. Total silence was mandated at that time.

Despite that edict, the loud snoring of twenty of the fifty former living on the street, alcoholics and drug addicts, was deafening. The smell of disinfectants was all encompassing. The whirr of ceiling fans served as a backdrop sound. There I was, inside my own skin frustrated with the impossibility of dropping off to sleep.

I would sometimes sneak off into the "library" a small room of Christian books twenty feet off the dormitory after "lights out." You were not supposed to but it was so blissfully quiet there. I would caress an old mothball-smelling quilt as my only comfort. Despite the fact that I was a six-foot person on a four-foot leather couch. I would mold my body to that space and immediately fall asleep. Only to just find REM when the night security guard would shine his flashlight in, telling me I must go back to the barracks. "Please let me stay," I begged, "I need to sleep." "I just can't do that bro." "Get back in your bunk."

Before going back to my bunk, I would put my face near the fish tank and watch the fish to kill any time I could, keeping one bleary eye on the breezeway clock for any movement closer to dawn.

At the farm I learned that you could get used to anything if you have no choice. I was not, however, getting used to being tortured by my own condemnation. During these times I began to open to the possibility that this greater spirit, this all-encompassing Thing, had a purpose by doing this to me.

By staying awake I was forced to confront myself instead of being diverted from my thoughts. There would be no hiding from reality by sleeping. I used this time. It occurred to me during those long brutal torturous nights that there might be something worth saving in me. I did not know, until much later, from where I got the resolve and courage to look.

Farm life was a six-day work week starting at 5:30 a.m. A cold breakfast and some watery coffee was followed by a short walk to morning worship. It consisted of worship music and testimony and was held in the tabernacle, a ramshackle church complex that screamed poverty.

In the beginning I sat in the fourth pew on the end seat, as far away from other students as I could get and still be in the place. Scratchy speakers blared loud worship music. The loud music and defective speakers seriously irritated me. I tried to get as far from those blaring speakers as possible. After many months I started sitting with my brothers. The speakers no longer irritated me. In fact, I grew to like the music, and I began to know the place as special.

On weekdays we had class from 7:45 until 8:45 a.m. Then we went to our assigned work duty from 9 a.m. to 6 p.m. We had a half-hour lunch at noon with two ten-minute "smoke breaks" at 1 and 3 p.m. The farm served us donated food from unsold items collected from local supermarkets. It frequently was expired fare.

"Don't worry about that—it says the expiration date on it but that is only a suggested date" they told me. I thanked them for the explanation but I was always worried about that.

Free time was from six till eight forty-five then an end of day "pray out" and announcements in the "breezeway" till nine. They did not allow talking from 9–10 pm. They called it quiet time, to be used for contemplation, journaling and reading the Bible. I loved that hour. Then the lights turned off at ten.

I would typically wake up at 5 a.m. and lay in my bunk anticipating the shock of the fluorescent lights exploding like a chain reaction from one end of the barracks to the other at 5:30. Sitting on the edge of that harsh metal frame bed I got dressed in corroded sneakers, khaki pants and a t-shirt.

I would silently recite the Shepherd's Creed Psalm 23. I always paused on the verses "The Lord, is my shepherd I shall not want, and He restores my soul." I delighted in those thoughts and let those truths sink in every time. Like countless people before me, I found enormous comfort there. Change was coming but it was agonizingly slow.

◆

At first, my letters to Andy were complaining. I sought sympathy and assigned blame. They evolved into expressing what was in my heart. I was in the smoke-pit writing a letter to Andy. It was in my third month. It was half finished when the verses from a folk song from the sixties started playing in my heart, my soul.

I have never been a crier. That changed right then. I realized then what I had lost.

My sweet Andy

*There is always someone for each of us they
say and I need you forever and a day. We're
on a long journey so stay by my side... I have
to walk through this storm now so please be
my guide.*

*Andy, Forgive me for hurting you and putting
you through this hardship and separation.*

My change will be real, I promise you that.

*I don't know what the future holds. Whatever
it becomes it must have you in it.*

With love, Keith

I walked out into a vicious rain. No one saw my old
man tears.

◆

Andy began her letters by complaining about her
loneliness in Maryland and her accusations of fault.
Then one day, they abruptly changed and she wrote
the most beautiful words from her soul.

My Dear Keith

*I feel the change in both of us. In my
loneliness I began to ask myself why I love
you. I know I do. Since being apart I think of
what our love is made of and I treasure it.
With each letter that you write I see more*

and more why I love you. Find your faith and you'll find yourself.

Love Andy

I found great inspiration and comfort in the letters from Andy. Sometimes I would read those letters out loud in the smoke pit to the brothers. I was never embarrassed to do so. I've kept each one of those letters in a safe place. I did not keep them to remember those difficult days but to remember the kindness and encouragement she showed to that lost man.

Our trust was developing. It was unmistakable. It was real change. It was solid. I felt it. Every time I felt that trust from her, it made me feel I was on the right path.

◆

The People in Charge

The first morning at the farm I felt a fear of the men who were so different than me. I clung to a facade of superiority. Even though it offered little, it was my only protection. To say that I was off balance and insecure was an understatement. I didn't know who I was beside reciting the golf thing, the business thing and the places I've been. I didn't really have an identity besides those old experiences.

When I arrived that first morning the "house man" a burly troll-like, humorless man who oversaw the barracks greeted me with nothing but contempt and a superior attitude. He parroted the phrase that God had put him in a position of authority, and his orders were to be strictly heeded. It was obvious and I understood that this body of men needed to have structure and rules, but this man had no empathy or kindness whatsoever. Here I was, a college graduate, businessman and a smart person. How could God put a person like this in charge of me? His favorite phrase was "I do not care." He would roll his eyes and look up to the sky as if I were the biggest idiot God ever created, as if he were being tortured by my stupidity. I felt that surely there must be bigger idiots than me. Maybe he just hadn't run into one yet. Maybe, just maybe, the problem was him. He was the first of several in authority I encountered at the farm who held the power of his office like a club. These men who had never tasted any authority in their lives now had it over me. It made daily life difficult for me and it constantly humbled me, as if I hadn't been humbled enough by everything.

If all Faith Farm people had been like him, I could never have stayed. They were not. My job at the farm was as a receptionist at the front office. I answered phones, sorted mail, and greeted the occasional visitor to the office. It was here that I met a man that would profoundly affect my view of Christianity.

A thirty-something staff member at the Farm who frequently came into the office to retrieve his mail and spend time with me. He acted like he knew something I did not know. I really doubted that at first, but I came to realize that he really did know something I didn't. He was in no way cocky but there was a subtle look in his eyes. He never had to say it, but I sensed in him the inner confidence that I had been looking for since my competitive golf career. I wondered how he, a staff employee at a charity farm, had this apparent inner confidence and me, having done some things of note in life, had none. He impressed me as a man with no pretentions. He was confident in who he was as a Christian, and he was not apologetic about his beliefs.

At that time, I thought anyone talking about God and Christ should divert their eyes and somehow be ashamed of what they were professing. I told him I really do not know anything about Christianity and all this jabbering Christian speak was nonsense to me.

He said let me simplify this. Christ said, "Love me with all your heart and love your neighbor as yourself."

I asked him if that was all.

"Of course not, the more you know the better, but this is your start. Do this, recite the Twenty-third Psalm and the Lord's Prayer every morning."

I agreed to do that. I asked him where I could find this Psalm. "It's in the Bible, Keith." "Of course it is," I said.

We laughed together and a friendship began. This man showed me by his actions and how he carried himself that it is possible to love a stranger. He manifested a kindness, not always seen at the Farm. I wanted that kindness around me.

I was grateful for his kindness and his gift of a true starting point. In a place of such serious intent, we shared laughter, and I became inspired. He was medicine for my soul sickness.

He made me feel that even if the world were breaking down around me people like him would be there, it gave me heart. I thought if there was one person like him there must be more. I had to find them. I would look.

CHAPTER SEVEN

I learn some Christian language and a truth

I arrived at the farm having always ignored Christian teaching put before me. Faith Farm staff were skeptical. How was that even possible? Most people had at least a nodding relationship with Christianity. I explained that it was simply not important in my family.

I perceived religious people as naive types, not the intellectuals who I valued. For three years I attended an Episcopal prep school and went to chapel every school day. I cannot remember a single word spoken by the pastor there. I cannot even remember what he looked like. I can picture all my other teachers clearly. I also went to a Southern Baptist University for five years and attended some services there, but the results were the same as my previous school. I simply tuned out spirituality. I was purposely deaf and blind to it.

The teachers at Faith Farm began by using terms like repent, salvation, redemption, and forgive. The words meant nothing to me. They were simply propaganda to promote an ideology.

"Religion is the opiate of the masses" as Friedrich Engels claimed. I read that quote in college and bought it completely. I have always believed, for reasons I never understood, that I was somehow special. I did not need religion. My ego was enough.

My ego comforted me for most of my life. I knew what I knew, and that was it. My ego told me I was simply misunderstood, and people would catch on to how special I was. However, in those instances when people praised me, I never really believed them.

Knowing nothing of Christianity, I had resisted any thoughts since childhood. Having rejected the symbolism of the cross and Christ long ago. I was a lifelong atheist. I was my own god. My arrogance had shuttered that window through which I could have seen God. Again, I was my own god.

This seventy-three-year-old god, shuffled across that bridge on a late October day in Florida struggling to carry his duffel bag of wrinkled Polo clothes, fancy watch, and cellphone.

"You will get a chance here to change your identity," they said.

"Sure thing," I snickered under my breath, "how hard can that be?"

Being without distractions, no drugs, no outside world, no TV, or entertainment of any kind, had its own value. I had always had distractions. That distraction-free isolation was the perfect environment to explore myself even if I rejected this spirituality thing. So, it made sense that the experience might be beneficial. And, of course, I had nowhere else to go.

*

I did not know it at the time, but my journey began by confessing a truth. Truth, any truth, was a good thing for me. It made me hungry for more, for larger truths.

During my first week, I was assigned to the front office. Overseeing the switchboard, sorting mail, and directing visitors. During my first few days at the farm, I used the office phone several times to call Andy and my brother, thereby breaking a major rule. There is to be no phone use during the first thirty days here.

I was complaining on the office phone to my wife and brother about my sad situation, which I did frequently during those first few days. I was on the office phone and the assistant director burst out of his office and screamed at me "what do you think you're doing?"

I mumbled some lies about having to make some arrangements with family. He asked me if this was the first time I had used the office phone.

Yes. I lied.

He scrolled through the phone's history and saw my previous calls to my wife and brother.

"Not only did you betray our trust, but you just lied about it." He asked me why I lied.

In my past I would have minimized and deflected the issue to defend myself. I was, however, totally exhausted from lack of sleep and detoxing so without thinking I spit out the truth.

"Keith, why did you just lie to me?"

"Look Charlie, I have manipulated and told lies all my life easily and without compunction. Sure, people had known me to lie but did not know I did it so often or easily."

It was day three and I made a confession out loud. I surprised myself by speaking the truth.

What I learned in that moment was that I had never valued truth. Was this place starting to work? Can it actually work? It was a start.

the farm program

The farm's year-long "regeneration" curriculum focuses on finding a personal relationship with God and culminates with the inner healing phase. In my mind, all classes up to that point were simply preparation for the inner healing phase. The sequence concluded with a final phase of much-needed and welcomed decompression.

A requirement for every student was to understand and practice the two major principles of gratitude and forgiveness, or risk not advancing on through the five phases. While practicing these principles, I certainly changed. To be fair, I think everyone did. From this practice, I learned to forgive the slights and failures, old and new, by which I had defined myself. Some of these slights and failures were perceived, and some were real. It was not important to distinguish between the two. These perceptions give us the perspective through which we make our life choices and form our self-view. I slowly lost my resentments and learned that I could forgive myself as well as others. It was a stupendous, freeing high.

They say, "God cannot bless the man we pretend to be." Who was I pretending to be? I asked many times. When I got my answer, I sought change. It was an honest search. I began to open to the possibility that this greater spirit this all-encompassing God knew there was something in me worth saving just as Andy had known what that greater thing was, but it still remained vague and unclear to me. I did not know, at first, where I got the resolve and courage to look.

Journaling, writing to Andy and occasionally getting a good night's sleep were my only solace during the endless days and nights of the farm. Days piled on top of days, indistinguishable from one another. The night's journaling was so different.

A requirement was for each student to keep a daily journal to commune with God by asking questions and writing answers. I was skeptical at first. Was God replying to me or was my own conscience writing the answers? In time the answer to that question became clear. I came to know God through my journals.

Each day we were to write five things to be grateful for and five people to forgive. Then we were to tell God our concerns and ask questions by entering them in a prescribed journal format.

◆

My Journal

My journal was the vehicle through which God introduced Himself to me and gave me comfort. He showed me the reason for my life dissatisfaction was a soul sickness, and He was the only one who could heal me. I learned my soul could and should direct my intellect, not the other way around. That was a huge insight for me.

If I were to be healed and then changed, I had to completely empty the corruption of my old self. I had to let God fill my empty soul with His loving spirit. God would not grace my corrupted soul. I had to completely open my heart. My first journal entries went like this.

> *God, I do not know if anyone is reading this but me. I feel doubtful, but the people here tell me you are listening. I am skeptical, but I will do the exercise. If you exist, please show me. I need something direct, clear. No vague words or expressions. I have never seen you. Show me. Prove yourself to me. Get me out of here.*

There was no response. Of course there wasn't, but I tried again.

> *They tell me you are a loving God. If so, how could you have let me stumble through my life for seventy-three years without revealing yourself, knowing my confusion, pain, and the harm I have caused others?*

The pencil in my hand moved, and the words appeared before me. Believe me, reader, when I tell you the writing of His replies was not conscious. The words seemed to write themselves. I simply read them.

"Keith, I tried to reach you many times. I was with you when you saw your son for the first time, and you cried in awe. I tried when you saw Victoria Falls in Africa, and you were awed by the thunderous vibrations from that waterfall. I know you felt Me there with you. I was there when that drug dealer determined he was going to kill you. He miraculously found money you had hidden in your car and long forgotten. He spared you. I was there many times, but you could not see Me. Keith, your eyes were closed. You were a closed-minded person infected by your belief that comfort, pleasures, and security were the only things of value in your life. You let your ego control your life's decisions. What was once a pure soul was corrupted over time. What I created as the 'real' Keith, you corrupted. I forgive you. This is your chance to change."

OK, that is powerful stuff, but I am asking for proof. Please tell me who You are. What are you?

"I am a pure love, and you cannot conceive of my being, accept me or do not. You have the will."

How do I know if what I hear from you is true?

"Carefully listen to that voice inside of you. That voice is me speaking from your soul, not your mind. I am within you."

I have listened to a voice all my life. The voice that I listened to eventually got me into this situation. How will I know the difference between that voice and Yours?

> *"You will come to know the difference on the journey that I have put you on. I promise that the truth will reveal itself. I promise that. Listen from your soul not your mind."*

What do you want from me?

> *"I want you to have clarity."*

There must be more.

> *"Love Me and have faith. Trust that my guidance is true and that I will keep my promises."*

Why would You, an all-knowing omniscient God even concern yourself with me? Put simply, I am a nonbelieving, broken old man, in bunk 42 in a barracks of losers in Boynton Beach homeless camp?

> *"Keith, I know who you are better than you do. I am here with you in bunk 42. If you believe, I will always be with you. That is who I am. They are not losers."*

You are giving me hope for my future.

"No. I am not giving you hope. I am the living hope. I will live with you and in you. Have clarity to understand that."

My mind has always been disorganized and unaware, clouded by a filter of self-doubt. That filter causes me to hesitate before I speak or act. I would like to respond freely from the person I am. Can I change into an honest person?

"Speak from your soul. Change is why I brought you here. Ask me each day for clarity."

I will. Please help me, stay with me.

There were many nights like that. I finally knew there was a God. I was no longer an atheist. I encountered Him each night in my bunk under my blanket writing to Him by flashlight. He saved me from despair. There was no doubt in my mind about His existence. I spoke with Him each night, and He gave me comfort and direction. I only asked God for one thing during my time in Faith Farm: clarity of mind. God promised me that if I had clarity all else would be revealed to me and it was. And so it went, night after night, for ten months. I asked God and He answered.

In the beginning I asked softly, self-consciously for forgiveness to God, who at first, I only hoped was listening. Then with confidence. I shared the most personal shames and hopes I carried within. I do not know why He spoke with me, I only know He did.

During these nightly revelations I began to heal. He lifted my lifelong depression and anxiety. He restored my soul. He gave my mind the clarity I sought for but never knew how to find. My healing and transformation were both brutal and beautiful at the same time—brutiful. During those endless days, my emotions were on steroids. The days were long and brutal. At night, God's voice in my journal would calm me. I rested in Him. It was beautiful.

After a few of these eye-opening nightly sessions, I began to pray, mainly expressing my gratitude. I never asked for comfort, success, or any favors. I began and continued to ask for only one thing: clarity of mind. God gave that to me, and I thank Him for that every day.

I read once and I believe that if the words you say in a prayer come back to echo in your heart, then your prayer has been answered. My heart began to echo and still does—every day.

CHAPTER NINE

not them but us

The men at Faith Farm were mostly exhausted men. They were not strong enough to continue fighting a battle against a world; they genuinely believed, deep inside, that they cannot win. They needed to rest. Many had just given up. Their experiences with jails, prisons, hospitals and rehab facilities always made them feel lesser than. Their perception of their life experience gave them an identity that would eventually kill them. They needed to rest and while taking that rest some found inspiration and hope. Could they even conceive of another identity, a true one, separate from the past? Could these "not needed people" change? That was the question. Some could and did.

All men who came to Faith Farm were broken people in every sense. There were no moderately broken people. Some kept to themselves and kept their secrets buried. That was such a sad thing. There were others who could show love even while looking up from the hole they were in. I sought these men out and had beautiful talks with them in the smoke pit. Others mourned their lost lives. We talked positivity into each other. We were offering hope to one another. We were homeless, drug addicted, mentally, and physically sick, abandoned by loved ones, resentful of society and frequently in jail, prison, or hospitals. We found ourselves in a place that was a depository of not needed things and people. We were all not needed people. We had that in common.

The farm put non-needed things in the store for resale and people in the barracks. We not needed people banded together and talked with absolute honesty to each other. We became stronger for it.

Most of my fellow students had backgrounds of abandonment, abuse, or major trauma. I was so different from them in that way. I was an entitled man. My life situation had shielded me from the ugliness that was typical of a Faith Farm life story. They had a sadness one deeper than the next. I thought I had little in common with them. At first, I held myself aloof. After living close to them for a time, I began to think not of them and me but of *us*. I looked at us as who we were, stripped of all superficial identities, badges, and labels. That was Faith Farm, the beauty of that place. My ability to understand that was the direct result of the clarity that God gave me. That lesson I learned about people was worth the price of admission and all the hardships and indignities I endured.

◆

The houseman assigned bunk 34b to a new arrival. It was three bunks down from me. A handsome fifty-year-old moved into the bunk with its small plastic olive-green dresser. He was a heroin addict who just by his looks would have been my friend in another superficial world. A heroin addict who came to the farm trying to hide the most horrible internal scars I had ever seen.

Internal scars are abundant on the farm. Most have them but he was world class infected. He was unusual even for Faith Farm. His calm warm brown eyes stared steadily, showing nothing of his hurt. He was good at hiding his shame. He maintained eye contact, but he did not use that affectation to let others know about him. He used eye contact to throw others off his real state of mind. It was a false calmness that in no way showed the calamity of his life. Life had been taken from him, and he used eye contact as a kind of makeup to disguise himself. I had never known a totally empty shell of a person. He walked and talked but there was nothing there.

His snoring was by far the loudest of any in the dormitory of loud snores. It was incomprehensibly loud and kept me awake night after night. I have always been sensitive and irritated by snoring. His snoring reminded me of a time I heard a trapped animal in its death throws, but louder. Throwing shoes and anything else at him had no effect. For a full month I was unable to sleep. His snoring grated every nerve in my body. The only day we were able to take a nap was Sundays. When the chance arose on a

Sunday just as I would close my eyes his concert began. I hated that guy with every fiber of my body. My hatred of him lived in my head. He must have felt it because he made it clear that the feeling was mutual. He constantly mocked me like a bully on the playground. When I talked about my golf career, he would tell me that it really was boring. Nothing about my life was interesting or done correctly. He showed his resentment toward me in everything he did. He saw how unsure I was of myself and picked on me constantly like a scab on a fresh wound. He delighted in upsetting me. I hated him.

I tried to take into consideration that most of us were defensive. We were trying to protect our vulnerable selves. I had the same defenses after all. I saw those elements of myself in him. It was also the way he carried himself or how he spoke about certain things. The reflection disgusted me. I learned to deal with that hatred of both him and me by practicing the Christian principle of forgiveness. It took me several months but only by forgiving both of us could I understand him. I forgave both myself and him. I came to understand the power of that action.

I came to know him. He confessed to losing his wife after providing her with the drugs that killed her. The state took away his two young children. He conned money from the family business to support his heroin addiction. His family disowned him. He had been in and out of numerous jails and rehab facilities.

I came to understand his pain. I tried to show him kindness and empathy. Slowly he responded to that.

I came to love him like a brother. I understood. He was just like me. When we talked it was without pretention. It was true.

CHAPTER TEN

I become a Christian

My epiphany came in the third phase of the program. During this ten-week phase our group of six men was isolated from the community in a separate housing section.

We served as acolytes at the church services and were frequently brought into the service to testify as to what God was doing in our lives. We were living in a way few of us had known before being at the farm. We had three hours of intensive class, went to work, ate in a separate place in the dining hall and were required to have an "accountability partner" wherever we went. We were given permission to stay up well past barracks lights out and frequently had only four to five hours sleep per night. We lived cheek to jowl, totally absorbed in the task at hand 24/7 for ten weeks.

My first thought was that I knew what they were doing. I had been through basic training in the army. I knew about the process of sleep deprivation, breaking a person down, then building him up again in the new desired image. My ego initially resisted. It told me I knew their game, and I was too smart to be manipulated. I was called out about my attitude by the brothers one night. They later recalled that a switch was turned on and I began to speak only bone-jarring honesty for the rest of the phase, to my benefit.

Ten weeks of intense focus in a room we lived in, except for sleeping, eating, or working. We read aloud our expanded journals each night, critiquing them among ourselves. We aggressively called out dishonesty, deflection or attempts at manipulation. We read them the next day in class, with the Pastor suggesting questions to ask God in our journals for the next night. The theme was, get naked before God.

We were getting at the previously unknown, suppressed beliefs we carried that had caused our self-destructive actions. We would each draw out impactful events and the belief drawn from that event on a blackboard.

By speaking these things and looking at them objectively, I began to see the harm was not solely in the trauma but rather the belief coming from those traumas. Often these beliefs were misguided because they were seen through the eyes of a child. A trauma was experienced, a belief came from it, impressed and embedded for a lifetime. Seen from the present perspective, I reevaluated, looking from the person I was now. I saw the value in correcting false beliefs. I saw it with each of my brothers and then finally in myself.

Although my issues were not any conventional traumas, they were painful, nonetheless. My personal false beliefs will remain in that room as will my brothers. I will share one thing: my father's death. During the last twenty seconds of my father's life as he lay on his bed he turned to look directly into my eyes. He held that look for several beats. Whatever he was looking for he did not see it. Without a word, he turned away from me to look at my mother and he died. I believed that what I saw was a father's disappointment in his son. I took away a belief from a dying man's glance. I had reconciled with my father and knew he loved me, but that glance haunted me. I worked through that false belief and found relief. Relief is not a strong enough word for the transformation that my brothers and I experienced there. The better word was freedom. Freedom from the negative beliefs that had shaped our lives.

◆

The Pastor

The Head Pastor of the farm conducted the third phase. He was a large Puerto Rican man who wore a kindness born of suffering. He presented sternness but was quick to break into a smile.

He showed his love for broken people openly and easily. This Pastor had complete and total commitment to his purpose which was to use God to heal broken souls. To him, addiction was not the root problem but another symptom of a damaged soul. He was there to minister to the broken. Watching and listening to him closely, my cynical self looked for any kind of pandering or ulterior motive. During the many hours I spent in that room with him I saw only a total sincerity I was not familiar with. My cynical nature changed from his example. I gained profound respect for him and the work he performs. He led me to Jesus.

My convincing Christian experience came after several weeks in his class. During one class I found myself standing in the middle of the room with my brothers seated around the perimeter.

The Pastor asked "Keith, do you believe Jesus is the son of God and He was crucified and resurrected for our sins?" I could not say yes. I knew without question that there is a God by that time but I was not certain about the rest.

The Pastor said, "let us get right to the point."

He said, "there is a door right in front of you. Take it!" All my instincts shouted, it was a fake. I was being manipulated. "Keith, do you believe that God can do anything?" Then "let Him." I let God. I was somehow transformed into that reality and saw an ordinary-looking door. I turned the knob and walked through it. There was God as Jesus, alive, smiling at me with his arms open wide. I looked directly into His eyes and I saw for the first time what true kindness is. I tried to go towards him, I wanted to embrace Him but I could not move. I tried to speak but I could form no words. I stared directly into those warm, knowing eyes of pure love. He continued to look directly at me. The next thing I knew I was back in that classroom. I had no doubts after that. There never will be. I am an unapologetic Christian believer. That day was worth enduring every indignity the farm had to offer. I have never had a life experience as powerful, not even close.

By the end of ten weeks of grueling classes I realized my previous relationships were superficial. There was just no depth in my relationships with people. My old self existed without a living soul, had no scruples, or ethics. I lied with impunity. I saw every relationship as transactional, what could they do for me. I saw what non-superficial interaction looked like in that class. I learned to express myself from my soul and not my ego. My previous reason for existing was to protect my ego. God would not relate to the person that I had created. I needed to be the person that God created. Finding confidence was what I had hoped for beginning my search. Finding God was the solution. It was the answer to my lack of inner confidence. I could never have created that confidence but it was always in me to find.

After a year I completed the program and was given a diploma. I made a little speech at graduation. I had graduated from a prestigious prep school, a university, and from several other noteworthy programs. I had received diplomas and such. Those documents which I no longer have never gave me a sense of accomplishment. My certificate from Faith Farm hangs in my office. I have profound respect for anyone who has finished the course at Faith Farm. Officials of the farm have told me I am the oldest man to graduate the Farm in seventy-six years. I know that if I can do it anyone can. If they are willing. That is the rub.

CHAPTER ELEVEN

I look back

I am thinking of all the blessings I enjoy now. There are really too many to count. There have been many tears shed—old man tears—no longer shed of desperation but now of joy. The joy I feel can be overwhelming. Andy and I are together again after two and a half years. It is as if we were never apart. My brother and I are as two old men sharing our past, as only brothers can. I have no resentments, anxieties, or depression. I have this incredible mental clarity. I'm able to work in a high intensity brokerage office as a seventy-six-year-old man and write at night.

God walked me through the fire of Faith Farm. He gave me a trial and the inner strength to succeed so that I would discover who He made me to be. Jesus put His presence right in front of me so that I could not miss seeing Him. Taken together, these became the tools for my content and rewarding life. I am living that life today—and every day.

As I walked out over the bridge the last time, I took stock of myself. In that year, my soul was restored to its original manufacturer's condition. I did not fear dying. I am a calm person. I know what real love is. I am not anxious, depressed, or addicted to anything. I have clarity of mind. What gifts He gave me.

There was profound change in me, yet I did not have my wife, brother, or son back. I was dead broke with no financial prospects. No one in my past life would rescue me. The fact that I was not troubled by those realities made me laugh out loud.

I thought of a journal question that I had asked God: *God, what does my future hold?*

God replied that He would not harm me and that He would prosper me. That was all I needed. I understood I was carrying within me the true importance in life. It was God's Grace. It would always be with me if I looked to Him. A thought struck me, and I got chills.

In thinking about the man who walked in over that bridge. I felt as though I was so alone. I never truly was—and would never feel that way again. My smile came easily. I quickly picked up my bags and got on the bus for the Fort Lauderdale Tabernacle, where I would put my life together. I would set new goals as a new man—a serious man, with clarity. Maybe I'll even try to author a story I thought. I was eager to start this new life.

It had been a brutiful year, both brutal and beautiful. I thank God every day.

ABOUT THE AUTHOR

Keith Stuhler is a former Class A PGA golf professional whose career in the sport spanned decades and continents. He competed and taught across Johannesburg, Tokyo, Singapore, Hong Kong, Europe, and extensively throughout North America, winning the Danny Kaye Open along the way.

Beyond the course, he built a diverse business career that included serving as CEO of a golf simulator company headquartered in Silicon Valley, Senior Associate at Laventhol & Horwath, President of Hole in One Properties, President of the World Indoor Golf Association, and publisher of a nationally circulated newsletter on golf simulation technology.

Keith founded The Children's Golf Foundation, a program dedicated to making the sport accessible to children with special needs. First Tee, one of the most recognized youth development organizations in golf, helped fund the initiative. The foundation continues in operation today.

A graduate of St. Bernard's Preparatory School with a university degree in Russian Studies, Keith brought an unconventional intellectual background to an industry built on tradition.

Today at seventy-six, Keith lives in Pompano Beach, Florida with his wife Andy. He volunteers weekly feeding the homeless in downtown Fort Lauderdale and is available for speaking engagements related to addiction, recovery, and faith.

ABOUT FAITH FARM

Faith Farm Ministries is a Christian regeneration program for men and women struggling with addiction, homelessness, and life-controlling problems. Founded in 1951, Faith Farm operates residential programs across South Florida where participants live, work, and study in a structured Christian environment for twelve months.

The program is free of charge. It is funded entirely by donations and the operation of thrift stores throughout Palm Beach, Broward, and Okeechobee counties.

Keith Stuhler entered Faith Farm's Boynton Beach campus at the age of seventy-three and graduated twelve months later as the oldest graduate in the program's seventy-six-year history.

To learn more or to support Faith Farm's mission:

Faith Farm Ministries
9538 US Highway 441
Boynton Beach, FL 33472
www.faithfarm.org

READING GROUP GUIDE

1. Keith describes his public life as a carefully constructed facade. What are the warning signs that someone close to you might be hiding a struggle behind a successful exterior?

2. At seventy-three, Keith walked into Faith Farm as a committed atheist. What do you think made him open to change at that point in his life, and not before?

3. Keith calls his experience at Faith Farm "brutil", both brutal and beautiful at the same time. Can you identify a period in your own life that fits that word?

4. The journal conversations between Keith and God are central to the book. Whether or not you share Keith's faith, what did those passages reveal about the process of opening yourself to something you cannot control?

5. Keith writes that his soul was "restored to its original manufacturer's condition." What do you think he means by that? Is that kind of restoration possible for everyone?

6. Andy waited for Keith during his year at Faith Farm. What does her decision to wait tell you about the nature of love in long marriages? What would you have done in her position?

7. Keith became the oldest graduate in Faith Farm's seventy-six-year history. How does his age change the way you read his story? Would the book feel different if he had been thirty?

8. The title The Winter Planting suggests growth in a season when nothing is expected to grow. Where in your life have you experienced unexpected growth during a difficult season?

9. Keith writes that he "did not fear dying" after completing the program. What is the relationship between confronting your past and losing the fear of death?

10. If you could ask Keith one question after reading this book, what would it be? What would you want him to know about how his story affected you?

ACKNOWLEDGMENTS

To Micah, without whose love and encouragement nothing would have changed in me.

My many thanks to Teri Garland Bolinger, my editor, for her patience and her steady hand in shaping these pages into something others could follow.

To my friend Andrew, who read the draft and saw himself in it. His own life's hiccups gave him eyes for this story, and his expertise carried the book the final distance into something tangible people can hold in their hands.

And to my wife Andy. Words can never express what you mean to me and how your pure soul saw me through difficult times.

I love you.